30 MILES FROM J-TOWN

The Nicholas Roerich Poetry Prize is an annual first-book competition sponsored by the Nicholas Roerich Museum in New York City.

1988
The Volcano Inside by David Dooley

1989
Without Asking by Jane Ransom

1990
Death, But at a Good Price by Chris Semansky

1991 CO-WINNERS:
The Buried Houses by David Mason
Desire's Door by Lee McCarthy

1992
30 Miles from J-Town by Amy Uyematsu

Each volume of the Nicholas Roerich Poetry Prize Library is in print and available from:

Story Line Press
Three Oaks Farm
Brownsville, OR 97327

30 MILES FROM J-TOWN

BY AMY UYEMATSU

STORY LINE PRESS
1992

First American Printing

ACKNOWLEDGEMENTS
Grateful acknowledgement is made to the following magazines in which a number of these poems first appeared: *AMERASIA JOURNAL*, "Did You Hear What Happened to Mo?","Near Roscoe and Coldwater"; *BAMBOO RIDGE JOURNAL*, "Deliberate","Lexicon","The Old Woman Who Dances with Me","Inaka /Country Girl","Local Wisdom"; *CALIFORNIA STATE POETRY QUARTERLY*, "Nisei","Harvest", "I'll Start with the Premise of Black"; *CONTACT II*, "Mail Order","Lettuce and Strawberries"; *ECHOES IV*, "30 Miles from J-Town"; *EMBERS*, "A Recent Conversation with My Grandmother"; *FUSION*, "The Same Month They Bombed Cambodia"; *GREENFIELD REVIEW*, "Three Pulls of the Loom"; *HARBINGER*, "The Shaping of Pine"; *INVOCATION L.A.*, "Rice Planting"; *POETRY/LA*, "A Repeating Bass Line","Red Rooster, Yellow Sky","The Shizuoka-Ken Picnics","At Obachan's Funeral","Wintertide","From a Ceremony Repeated"; *RHINO*, "After Seeing a Film on Mishima"; *SCULPTURE GARDENS REVIEW*, "To All Us Sansei Who Wanted to Be Westside","The Garden She Tends","A Pinch of Bonito"; *SEATTLE REVIEW*, "San Kwo Low","Rock"; *TSUNAMI*, "I'm Told","From an Utagawa Print: Geishas Parading"; *WEST/WORD*, "Second Nature"; *ZONE*, "December 7 Always Brings Christmas Early"

This publication was made possible thanks in part to the generous support of the Nicholas Roerich Museum, the Andrew W. Mellon Foundation, and our individual contributors.

ISBN: 0-934257-92-2

Book design by Lysa McDowell

Published by Story Line Press, Inc.
Three Oaks Farm in Brownsville, OR 97327

for Chris

TABLE OF CONTENTS

SANSEI LINE DANCE

WAR STORIES

EVEN THE DYING WOMEN

MORE WAR STORIES

HARVEST

PARTIAL GLOSSARY

Certain Japanese words are used frequently throughout this volume. A partial glossary is provided below. Other terms may be indicated in footnotes.

sansei:	third-generation Japanese American
nisei:	second-generation Japanese American
issei:	first-generation Japanese American
hakujin:	Caucasians
nihonjin:	Japanese
ojichan:	grandfather
obachan:	grandmother
sashimi:	raw fish
gohan:	rice
maguro:	tuna
enryo:	sometimes interpreted as holding back
J-town:	Japan town, located in downtown Los Angeles
nihonmachi:	same as J-town
buddhahead:	slang term referring to Japanese Americans

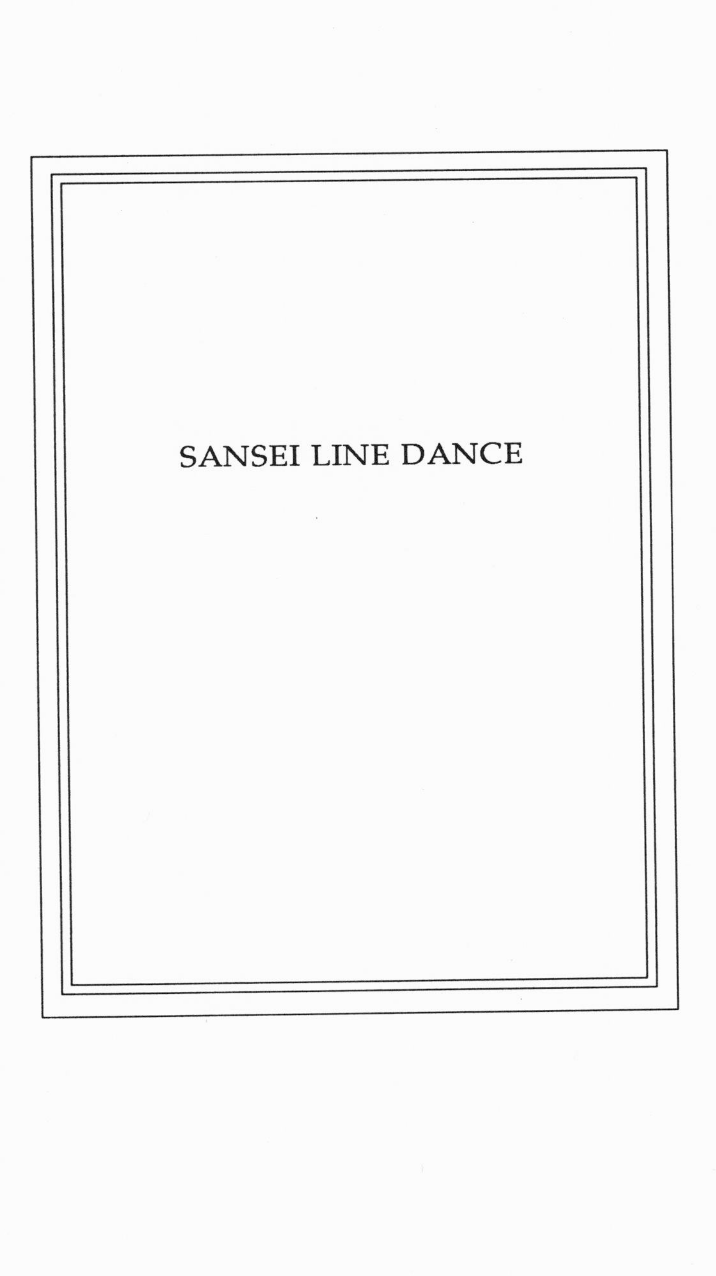

SANSEI LINE DANCE

TO ALL US SANSEI WHO WANTED TO BE WESTSIDE

It didn't matter where we lived
within a hundred miles of LA—
if you were Japanese growing up here
in the sixties, you weren't really buddhahead
unless you knew about the Westside,
Dorsey High School, dances at Rodger Young
followed by pork noodles at the allnight Holiday Bowl,
gangs called the Ministers, Baby Black Juans,
Buddha Bandits, and the boys who joined them
with the usual names, Kenny, Ronnie, and Shig.

By high school it was already too late for me.
I was from Pasadena and never got over
being forcefed a bleached blond culture
of cheerleaders, surfboards, red Corvettes,
lettermen's jackets I was never asked to wear.
Somebody had decreed the only places
you could stay Japanese and cool were the Westside,
Gardena, a few neighborhoods on the Eastside,
each with their own reputation—
hardly anyone from the outside ever got in.

This didn't stop me from hoping.
My sister and I made the long drive
into town on Saturday nights, thinking we'd get lucky,
get picked out of the crowded dance floor
by a pretty boy in a preacher jacket,

his hair in a 3-inch front,
so in profile everyone knew he was Westside
and could put on an almost black, southcentral strut
whenever he wanted to.

I guess you could say even I had my chances.
At least before they heard me talk,
I was often mistaken for a girl who'd been around,
I had that mature look—
imitated sansei chicks with ratted hair,
glued on eyelashes, shiny adhesive slivers
taping eyelids round like blackeyed lacquer dolls.
But as soon as a Westside boy
asked my name, where I lived,
I sounded just like any other hakujin,
"No, I'm not related to Billy Uyematsu,"
whose dad ran a fish shop on Jefferson and 8th,
no sense in lying when my lack of dialect
revealed too many years in white classrooms.
But I really gave myself away when we slowdanced—
no one had ever taught me how
a genuinely rowdy sansei could slowdance
though she barely moved her legs.

I envied Linda Watanabe who had gone
to my Sunday school. She was mean enough
to hang out in the bathroom at Parkview Auditorium,
eager to fight, along with the toughest Westside girls
amusing themselves as we scurried by.

Then she started going out with blacks
and our parents told us to stay away.
When Linda got pregnant, her family said
she was going to visit her relatives in Japan.
It became a frequent inside joke,
another sansei daughter spending her summer
back in the old country.

I never got my Westside boyfriend
though I acquired a permanent taste for romance,
dark men, harmonizing to groups so smooth
only they could get away with calling themselves
the Stylistics, Flamingos, Delphonics,
Rosie and the Originals.
I went to concerts where *we* were the majority,
like the time Mike Sato from Gardena
took me to hear Smokey sing, "Ooh, baby, baby,"
long before it was a Ronstadt remake,
or I danced to "Are you angry with me, darling"
as the real Little Willie G. of Thee Midnighters
stood no more than ten feet away.
And now, over twenty years later,
when I meet other sansei, they'll say,
"Didn't you grow up on the Westside?"—
and a girl doesn't get asked that
unless they think she's got some degree of cool.

30 MILES FROM J-TOWN

1

dad was a nurseryman
but didn't know that sansei
offspring can't be ripped
from the soil
like juniper cuttings.

2

we were fast learners
we spoke with no accent
we were the first to live
                    among strangers
we were not taught to say
                    ojichan, obachan
                    to grandparents
we were given western
                    middle names
we collected scholarships
                    and diplomas
we had a one word japanese
                    vocabulary:
                    hakujin
                    meaning: white
it became my dictionary.

3

and in the summer when
    girlsmooth cheeks turn mexican brown
we were given the juice of a lemon
    an old country notion, its sting should return
    us to our intended feminine selves

4

if you're hip in l.a. you eat
sashimi at least
once a month you know
the difference between
fresh and saltwater eel you cultivate
a special relationship with one
sushi chef you call
each other by first names-san.
as for me
I had sashimi on hot august nights
steaks grilled rare, 5 cups steamed gohan,
maguro never mushy sliced thick red,
and while the tongue burns sweet
from the mustard of wasabi,
mom brings in wedges
of moist chocolate cake
for cooling.

5

they didn't force the usual
customs on us.
no kimonoed dolls in glass cases
no pink and white sashes
for dancing the summer obon
we weren't taught the intricacies
of folding gold and maroon squares
into crisp winged cranes, but
we never forgot enryo
or the fine art of speaking
through silences.

6

every two or three years america goes asia exotic
        rising sun t-shirts and headbands
                rock stars discover geishas and chinagirls
and asian american women become more desirable
        in fashion
                almost a status symbol   in some circles
be careful it doesn't go to our heads
in videos blond hero always rescues us from yellow man.

7

quickchange sansei
we can talk cool whether we're from
southcentral lincoln heights or the flats
and even when we're not
we can say a few pidgeon phrases
a crude japanese english
offered to grandparents
before they die,
we can fool
sound just like an american
over the phone,
and in public places
we usually don't talk at all.

8

on important occasions
dad drove us into j-town
through the eastside barrio
past the evergreen cemetary
his sister and brother
never knew manzanar
kanji and english inscribed
on their gravestones
then over the first street bridge
into nihonmachi

this was the center
this was the lifeline

9

I go to japanese movies
whenever they come to town
      curious I see few and fewer like me
there are muscular young black men
and white men with indoor complexions
      some don't even need subtitles
      but they cannot know

I have to be here
I must spend these three hours
      with faces voices
      warriors farmers lovers
I would know
and to my soul
      these quivering notes
      of the shakuhachi
melodies I have heard long ago

10

grandma morita had no time
to learn how to drive the machine
but she took us by bus
to woolworth's
a dollar each to buy treats
for two girls who could never
talk to her about dreams.

A REPEATING BASS LINE

first.

wisteria & jacaranda

grew wild
        through our town, their
lavender and blue blossoms
        fell lightly, made
a cool shade of fuji iro,
        wisteria purple,
but I felt the whispers
        and men who won't smile
        at the children we were,
our grandfathers
        tending the land
long before the flight
        of citydwellers
        three bedroom families
and artists who moved into
        canyons of boulders and pine.

sierra madre used
        its natural beauty
tried to make us forget
        lima avenue for jews,
grove street
        for mexicans and japs,

wisteria & jacaranda
grew wild there too.
and one night we watched
a flame burn
blue purple
on the lawn down our street.

but the next day only
a scorched outline
that creeps into dreams
and soon the grass
grew full again.

second.

I had to take
shallow breaths the pepper trees
and long leaves of eucalyptus
filled the air
a sticky sweetness

I waited
for the last warm days of autumn
the slow beat at dusk
after santa ana winds

depended on the light shift
purple touching blue
in the san gabriels behind me

and tints
of the palest coral
an indian turquoise   a mikan
ripe with orange
opening the borders.

third.

there was that brief city time
no purple bush
or petal
the best I could do
cut squares of cloth
lilac fuchsia burgundy
assorted crisp cottons
a few silk patches
faded and handdyed from
the old country
search for the right hue
a scarf of purple
against gold
on a buddhist shrine
or the smooth skin
dark like the satsuma
gather the squares.
toss them.
let them fall.
lines to prints
florals to japanese

geometrics. toss them
again, a repeating
nonsymmetry.
finally piece them
into a huge futon
to wrap myself
through winter.

I've brought the quilt
to this town built on desert
too dry for wisteria.
no better or worse.
in sandy soil
I planted a plum tree
since spring its branches
are full, turning
slowly into
the shade of blood
and by birth
the last tree
to lose leaves in winter.

RED ROOSTER, YELLOW SKY

The grandmother who never spoke
brought me this card from Japan
drawn in a child's hand:
just rooster, sun, and sky.
Under a red sun
the rooster's red body
splits in two uneven parts,
each sturdy black foot
holding its own weight.
It was the year of the rooster
when I was still ten,
learning to stand myself upright—
my own sky rising yellow
like new, uncut lemons.

DELIBERATE

So by sixteen we move in packs
learn to strut and slide
in deliberate lowdown rhythm
talk in a syn/co/pa/ted beat
because we want so bad
to be cool, never to be mistaken
for white, even when we leave
these rowdier L.A. streets—
remember how we paint our eyes
like gangsters
flash our legs in nylons
sassy black high heels
or two inch zippered boots
stack them by the door at night
next to Daddys' muddy gardening shoes.

AFTER SEEING A FILM ON MISHIMA

There are some of us
who trace samurai
in their bloodlines,
just lately reveal
authentic family crests
on mantles & custommade stationery,
pay $250 to have their genealogy
bound and passed on.
They forget how
the samurai shielded
his hands in steel and silk.
Hands that can't last
a week's plowing the Imperial Valley.
Or a month behind the barbed wire
of Manzanar and afterward
to start counting time
as if from the first day.
Then the raking and bundling,
weeds into years,
in the white man's backyards.
In samurai legends
a man saved his honor
with the ragged pull of blade
through bowels.
Our grandfathers would trade his sword

for twelve infant pine trees,
matsu for shaping,
each night after the washing away
of sweat and dust.

---

matsu: pine tree

THE SHIZUOKA-KEN PICNICS

I step into the line dance
winding its path
down East First Street
this hot August evening.
I am the woman
who wears her kimono loosely,
unpowdered neck
and unbound breasts,
my sash tied lightly
around my hips.
These arms swing too wide
as I move disjointed,
trying to remember
the samisen women.

As a young girl
I would climb the steep trails
of Elysian Park hills,
then lie at the base
of their grassy slopes,
sun on my tanned brown face.
I watch all who gather
for the kenjinkai picnic—
my grandfathers,
still in their fifties,
unwinding the red and white Shizuoka
banner across the small stage,

the wives unrolling tatami mats
under the shade,
while four pale young women
dance two in a line—
their slight angle of head,
eyes following an uplifted arm.

I know this small gesture—
the held silence
before their next turn.
But the sun is so warm
and I am impatient.
I rush toward the cool eucalyptus trees,
find a hiding place
in the long leaved branches.
Here I wait for the dancing to end,
though all around me
the distant sound of a Japanese song,
a light drumming far past these hills.

---

samisen: a 3-stringed Japanese musical instrument
kenjinkai: association of Japanese immigrants from the same prefecture or province in Japan
Shizuoka: kenjinkai where Mt. Fujiyama is located

SAN KWO LOW

The San Kwo Low sign was taken down
years ago and if this city has its way,
I'll forget about those Sunday dinners,
the quick drive from Montebello to J-town,
the shortcut we took through a dark alley
to get to the restaurant,
our thin legs running toward the lights
of East First Street and my nightmares
about men who hide between buildings.
Mary and I wore Grandma's latest matching
dresses, made of polished cotton with ribbon sashes.
In our patent leather shoes, we climbed
the long flight of linoleum steps,
looping past the men who dined alone
at the narrow first floor counter.
We always ate upstairs.
The Chinese waiters greeted us in broken English,
guiding us to our compartment.
Behind dark rosewood partitions
we sat hidden from other families,
adult voices hushed behind thin wooden panels.
I want to remember their conversations—
the sound of Grandpa's voice,
but instead I hear the waiters gathered
by the kitchen laughing and talking in Cantonese,
the constant clatter of dishes and pans,

spoiled Japanese sons running
the length of the dining room,
flashing their arms and legs
between partition openings,
catching glimpses of black hair,
orange Nehi soda and smiling old women.
We held every imporant Morita event there
but now I can barely recall what it looked like.
I need evidence that we were once
a family which cherished its connections
through the immigrant grandparents.
I miss that commotion of chairs
pushed back from the table all at once,
as our three generations finished another meal
and left knowing we'd be coming back.

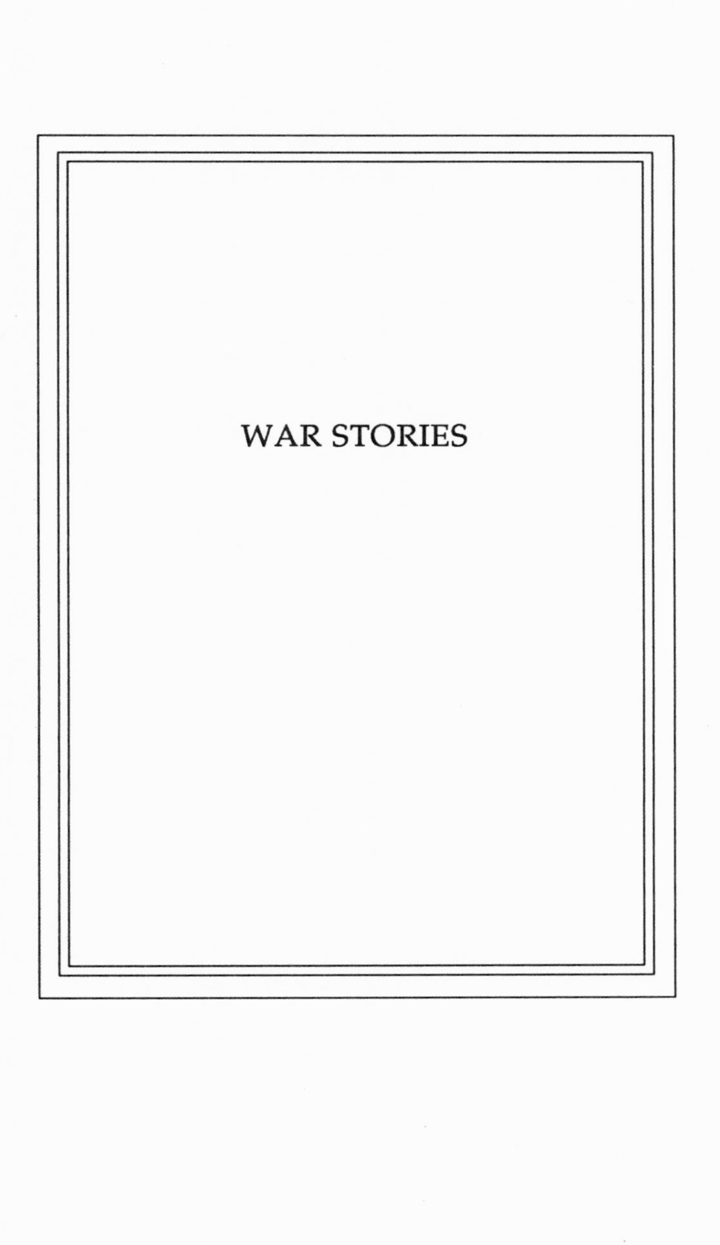

WAR STORIES

SECOND NATURE (or Lessons on Beauty)

In America it begins
with the geometry of skin—
how to enter a room
count the number of windows
for escape
in daydream my fingers
retracing the rounder shape of an eye
which doesn't fit mine.

Some walls have a brightness
which suck the color yellow
back into itself,
if I become invisible
everyone else can keep smiling.
Other walls collapse
from the rising noise
of my own unwantedness—
as I walk through a restaurant
or my high school dance
and no one but me
hears their talking stop.

I learn the safest way
to cross any sidewalk or living room—
do a fast count
of our ratio to whites.

I can spot other sansei
by the way we look sideways,
I'm too quick at exposing the lack
or definition of double eyelids,
like the way some men only turn
their heads toward blonds—
I always start with the size of our eyes.

But once on a crowded Tokyo street
when nobody notices—
my darker skin begins to breathe,
my black eyes take back their
original name,
I don't have to measure myself
against what I can never be.
All at once I am every woman again—
I sleep for twenty days
I pull every feature
back into my face.

DECEMBER 7 ALWAYS BRINGS CHRISTMAS EARLY

All persons of Japanese ancestry, both alien and nonalien, will be evacuated from the above designated area by 12:00 noon.
— Executive Order 9066, Franklin D. Roosevelt,1942

december 7 always brings christmas early
in neat white packages
red circles perfectly centered
one to a side

mama was taken away in a long railed box
blinds pulled taut to hold in her shame

they delivered her to a box in santa anita
walls lined with tissue paper hay
layered over manure and the bloody vomit
that gushes from caged animals

they confined her to a tarbacked box
in that flattened arizona desert
and in aerial photographs
the human cartons arranged row by row
framed by impeccably straight cornered wire borders
were picture perfect

they put me in an airless box
every december 7
when the history lesson was me

they gave me to babies
who were just learning the habits
of their fathers

forty years later the presents arrive
in one continuing commemoration
each precisely wrapped in black and white newsprint
houston st. louis new york
davis boston west philadelphia
in detroit the autoworker at the bar
didn't need to know the skull he smashed
belonged to vincent chin a name that didn't match

the evacuation of bodies resumes
judged by the same eyes that watched mama's train

NISEI

For my mother the waiting began
with train cars name tags baggage
assignments wire fences

they lined up for Gila and Rowher
Heart Mountain and Minidoka
Amache Jerome Manzanar Poston
Topaz and Tule Lake

they lined up every day
at mess halls and toilets
for showers a pledge of allegiance
army induction the endless
unanswerable loyalty tests.

ROCK

The sky is too white
here, clouds pressing
against granite
fill every crevice,
and breathless, our men
and women are sent away
to a desert named Manzanar,
close to a river gone dry.

Is this where dark
collects light, along the edge
of each rock still holding
the path of one river,
stone guiding stone,
where our men
will forget how to talk
as they climb
the huge boulders and watch
their youngest children
racing into open
pockets of the riverbed,
choosing only the smoothest
pebbles, pure black ovals,
light enough to carry
back in small hands.

How many more years
before we can hear the cool
rush, a desert rain
that keeps gathering inside us
but stays hidden
in the silence of fathers.

Manzanar, a relocation camp for Japanese Americans during World War II, means "apple orchard" in Spanish.

WAR STORY

once I was angry with you
for letting them take you away.
grandpa, veteran of one world war,
could even speak good english.
he helped them convince you
to go peacefully.
you could have yelled
burnt your homes
told f.d.r. to go to hell
or at least declared
your bitterness to me

once I was angry with you
for telling me only of the good times
two thousand nisei teenagers hanging out
in mess halls, canteens, by the north gunpost gate.
sneaking away to haystacks, a lovers' rendezvous.
see and hear each other all the time.
at school. next door. in the john. through the walls.
lining up. lining up.
did you know who went to the dance with who,
he's sure cute and does the darndest jitterbug,
mama was homecoming princess
but should've won,
anyone could tell from yearbook pictures,
gila class of 43.

once I was angry with you
bragging again about drinking one gallon of shoyu
to flunk the physical but you got drafted anyway
you went to italy and now you laugh every year
with the ones who came back.

---

gila: the World War II relocation camp my mother and her family were assigned to
shoyu: soy sauce

LOCAL WISDOM

it was just us nihonjin
at the blackjack table
with a dealer from hong kong,
so the nisei man from hawaii
who was sitting to my right,
sipping scotch rocks
to one hundred dollar bets,
summed it all up:

> "you know those white people,
> they always gotta make a lotta noise
> over nothin."

THE SHAPING OF PINE

1

for a lifetime
I did not speak
my grandfather's language
as a child
I could not see
his Japanese pine
touching my bedroom window
its branches clarified,
just three curves

slowly
against this setting
in white,
the pine has opened
through his hands.

2

I'm not sure when
I was taught
not to hear our talking
or if our talking
actually stopped.

some of us did choose silence
but this is different
from saying we were born silent.

by the third generation
I was sacrificed,
saved from broken tongues.
the grandmother who still survives
can no longer recognize me,
cannot pronounce my western name.
how can I ask her
to give me the lacquered red bridge,
repeated in haiku written
after she arrived.

3

with my child's eye
but without her quickness
I learn each word again

I want to begin here:

onna/ woman	kami/ god, or paper, or hair
kaze/ wind	oki/ big, or open sea
naka/ inside	me/ eye
ishi/ stone	yume/ dream.

4

afternoons on that grassy hill
I watch wind playing the bright weaves
which wrap the brown shoulders
of fishermen's sons

hidden I follow
the wind at dawn
a voiceless army awaits
waving its silken banners
each a silent movement of red

but when night fills
this pine forest
fire snapping to peasant drums
I dance the circle of women

from a western shore
the wind returns
breathing sadness
and carrying
each woman's laughter.

5

bachan sang lullaby
to my father

who forgets that once
he held me
tight in his arms,
singing a story
in Japanese rhyme,
now foreign sounds
which have split and resplit,
notes I must improvise
as I sing to my son

nen nen yo
baby in the snow
mommy gonna dakko you
hold you while you grow

after you cry
mommy hold the sky
mommy gonna let you go
baby gonna fly

after the snow
mommy gonna go
baby gonna sing goodbye
nen nen yo.

---

nen nen yo: Japanese sounds sung to me as a baby

dakko: to hold or embrace

6

we have our own legends here
kenjinkai gossip
huddling clan women
sorting out
the health and luck
of each offspring
and the wives who keep asking
about love

my mother admits
her own mother was crazy
blaming the great grandmother
who ran away with a lover
leaving the girl child
but taking the son

my other grandmother
was not the first wife
I've heard tales of fortune
and adultery
the first wife seen
being driven to Little Tokyo
where she met a musician
though she begged her husband
to stay here
she was shipped back
to our village in Shizuoka
then replaced.

7

when I watch our old women
I know this—

we have listened to our men die,
followed the course of tears hidden
as they wear disguises
for the white man
and often forget to remove them
for us.

we have carried the child
and the father,
holding the unwritten places
between heroes and war,
textbooks and medicine men.

our tools are simple.
lullaby. gossip. talkstory.
and what cannot be said,
passed on in rhythm,
gesture, and memory.

8

I came here from an island
my words replaced by hands and eyes

to you I only owned my hands
until you heard the sound they made on land
your fear concealed so carefully
you pretended that my eyes held secrets

I was forced into desert camps
where you didn't hear me counting what was stolen
and afterwards when I returned in silence
you even praised me

but I am talking now
a recent history
that you are still afraid to hear—
the issei you deported
nisei who refused
the rioters you shot
sons you sent away to fight your worst battles
and those of us who stayed behind

I am talking now inside our silence
after forty years of waiting
a nisei mother's public statement
the poems which could not be thrown away
and the grandfather who could never
take me back to Manzanar
where he rebuilt his garden
loud with sand, rock, and pine

I am talking to us now.

EVEN THE DYING WOMEN

AT OBACHAN'S FUNERAL

Even if I did not know her
I must say something,
for my own family is not unlike my husband's,
so much never said outloud.
He tells me that's the way it's always been
but I don't believe it.
It has more to do with the conditions of dying
in this country of hard light,
where the sky is too white and our men are not heard.
As the sun glares now through late morning fog,
it reflects our dark suited men,
women in black shoes.

My husband's mother, strongest
of obachan's four daughters,
has never let her children see tears.
But on this day she looks for her husband.
As all the women in her large clan watch,
she stands across from him,
only inches apart, hoping for his arms
to comfort her,
but she is asking too much.
I see the slightest shift in his eyes,
I'm sure all the women have seen it.
His arms never move.

An elder sister is ready
when my husband's mother finally cries,
grieving for what she's lost today
and for all that can't be buried.

THE GARDEN SHE TENDS

a bed of stones
all smooth and black
this late august night
when the wind
makes no sound
against them,
where a woman
remains as
if all the heat
from their past
summer rests here—
each stone
the singular shape
of a husband's eyes,
arms at his side,
even the simplest
words, cries
die under the taut
black surface
of a welltrained stare.
yet under each stone
it is moist,
as it always was,
and alone now
slowly she turns
one stone

in her hands,
holds the cool
wet silence
to her lips,
tonight a wife
knows her own form
of violence.

I'M TOLD

Nursery Grandma wrote haiku
won newspaper contests
hated crying babies.
In the 20's she had my father
driven to school, dressed him
in knickers, silk shirts,
patent leather shoes.

Her first husband beat her
so she was lucky
to get my grandfather,
who brought her to Los Angeles.
His speech was hard
and I'm told she married beneath
her class, but he knew how
to grow pink & white camellias,
hoped he could make everything
grow in his hands.
He built her a big house
hired nursemaids for their children,
so she could play the samisen
have time to write haiku.

She refused to learn English
never hugged us,
her only grandchildren.

She's outlived all the others,
won't leave the retirement home,
all her roommates are white
and her closest friends,
blue eyed nurses who bathe her
and like to call her honey.

Now when we visit she even hugs our children,
though she repeats herself in Japanese,
asking who we are as we kiss her goodbye.
I wonder how often she held my father.
How long will we wait
before he lets us kiss him again?
These are things I'm not told.

This is what I do know—
it was grandpa who sent postcards
from their trips back to Japan,
"love" handwritten
in his uncertain English.
But I have her thin wrists
and detect an inheritance
no distance could hide.

THREE PULLS OF THE LOOM

1. Immigrant

Years ago in a Japanese castle
my long hair sashed loosely
in silk and purple braid,
I carry messages between my lord's wife
and her lover,
I am the lady in waiting
I wait behind the shoji screen.
                    Or are these just the dreams
                    of every picture bride who came to this country.

Before she left Numazu
my grandmother was kept in her room,
in a time when a woman had one chance to marry
she learned that her body and his anger were one.
So it was arranged
she would go to California
live with a man whose first wife had already
been sent back.
                    In the locked room,
                    or sleeping next to my grandfather
                    who let himself master the touch and colors
                    of camellias, of these he was not afraid,
                    when did she learn to write haiku.

She was not like the farmers' wives
who coming in from the fields
held the small baby and later the grandchild.
She thought it enough that her husband
tracked mud into her bedroom.

And why do I write about this woman,
not the grandmother who played with me
my bachan who learned enough of the words
to say
in America, a girl can be anything she dreams.

2. Sisters

I look at the two nudes, lithographs Mary made
fifteen years ago. She was drawing us.
The larger nude, a white woman lying on her back,
her smile framed in a swirl of hair,
the roundness of body
repeated in the background
like leaves on water
or the tapestry print of the Moroccan pillows
in Mary's room.
I would visit her place
smell the incense and artist's paint
we drank jasmine tea.
We both knew the white woman,
the yearning that grows in young girls with beige skin
we had both learned what darkness can't bring,
but like sisters
we hurled our pain at each other.

Much later, we understood
it would be Mary who ran screaming
cursed the father
challenged the young men to watch her dance.

And I would visit her place, knowing
I was the other nude
a smaller print of a woman not completely inked in
my long feet moving on desert or beach sand.

There is a hole in my side
that Mary has not etched onto metal
so light breaks through on the blank surface
in the shape of a half moon,
the light almost breaks my body in half
and it's me at twenty
and it's us
and I have been healing the open side
a gentle hand
mine and for a time a man's.
We wove patches onto the broken skin
even when he did not know,
and here I am holding it up to the sun
letting it breathe in its own scent
though the white woman is always in my bed,
a third eye.

3. Maya

She walks down the highway
a narrow path through jungle
asphalt cemented against roots and vines,
green to the very edges.

She moves slowly,
but not resting thin arms and legs
she carries water or perhaps wood
for the noon meal.
As I go from the white man's cities,
wandering southward,
there are many like her.
But she has been waiting for me,
a brown woman
with eyes like mine,
the same high cheekbones.

The wet heat of Yucatan sun
pours into her brown face,
warms the lighter stretched skin
on breasts and belly.
The damp air is sweet,
dense with her odor which clings
to the forest just after it rains.
She calls herself the daughter of rain gods,
adorns her body in the cloud white dress,
the huipil that all women wear.

Even the dying women
who hold hands with the youngest children when walking.
And I too have nursed a child
remember the way my breasts ached,
the milk that flowed even before
he was sucking at my nipple.
I watch my rhythm in him now.
And I have cried with the rounding of many new moons,
blamed myself for the loneliness I've known,
but I see her now

she and all the women on the road,
adorning their bodies in the cloud white dress,
a soft canvas for weaving.

And into the garment's yoke
she has woven her own threads and shapes,
gathered colors from mangoes,
maize, quetzal plumes, and the gulf,
each daughter explaining her time and place
to the next woman,

so that I may know her.

THE OLD WOMAN WHO DANCES WITH ME

it all started about the same time
I became celibate.
as if everyone around me felt an energy
only I can provide them—
so now they all want to come to me
with their problems.
Sandy notices this too,
recognizing an unspoken calm
warns me about scavengers
inviting me to lunch
as if now I have more than enough
unused love to go around—
this is a power I don't welcome.
is it what draws confessors to a priest?

but damn it, even I can see I'm stronger
ran eight miles on Monday
don't cry nearly as much
go for weeks without convincing myself
I can live without a man.

lately I keep seeing the same old woman
wonder if I'm spending too much time
by myself. here she is again,
the fine white hair
straight to her waist

long fingers brown and tapered
silver rings on each hand.
she follows me everywhere—
as I wait at the bus stop
and before I fall asleep.

sometimes she is Japanese like me.
dances barefoot through a pine grove
wearing layers of white silk—
no sound of her feet
as she turns slowly toward me,
her teeth blackened.
then her skin turns darker—
she is outside the plaza
selling blankets and winter caps,
she does not know my language
though she finds me
when I daydream that field
of long mountain grass.
like her I have slender fingers
and use them to measure the length of my face
cheekbone to chin—
know my resemblance to her,
hear us walking together
once on the flat Manchurian plain.

I wonder if she still longs
to be held in a man's arms
and why she always smiles at me.

Nels told me what his friend saw
as she runs through my Yucatan poems,
blood no longer released
from her womb—
he feels her freedom.
I keep asking myself why an old woman
should accompany me now, when my own body
has barely begun to change,
when I just finished touching
the smooth skin behind a shoulder
and can still feel the easy fit of thighs.

but this old woman dances by herself.
maybe she wants to remind me
each of us dances alone.
I'm not afraid of this old woman
and will bring her oranges and tea.
here she is again—
a simple nod to my questions,
unable to keep her hands and feet
from rocking the sky.

A RECENT CONVERSATION WITH MY GRANDMOTHER

When I wake up in middream
or find myself humming
a melody with no sharps or flats,
I know I've been outside of this time.
If only I could speak with obachan,
not be groping inside this buried place
for the carelessly thrown out
language of immigrants,
only two generations
since leaving Shizuoka.
She knew I would go back to Izu peninsula,
climb the slopes of Omuro-yama
with my mother's cousin,
the wind slapping my hair
hard against my face,
no sound from the ocean below
as the wind moans
through the long mountain grass.

But I can't say the words.
We gave up a language well suited to farmers
and poets, its rhythm uneven with

brush stroke and pause.
It holds sound inside picture
with a thousand possibilities for
shadow and light.

Instead I must use
these words with no memory.

WINTERTIDE

Some part of me never left the snow country—
where my lover and I chase each other on a white mountain,
feeling nothing but our heat in the icy air,
where I have known the smell of fish broth and fire in the winter,
can remember standing by myself, surrounded by ice and sky,
not needing answers. There is a field of snow
where a woman can stand alone and hear everything.

I'LL START WITH THE PREMISE OF BLACK

1

where a fist or soft beak
startles into its own shape,
barely feeding itself from the dark womb,
a cave holding
no sound but this fluttering of bone
in still unlit waters.

2

a new morning gathers
within the black sky.
dawn begins tentative
then the pale mute pinks,
its slow tansformation
to an absolute light releasing
all the colors of my world—

but black is at the very center
of this sun rising to my opening eye.
I will always be that small cap
of wet, black hair
who entered like a gasp
through my mother's dark opening.

3

wherever I go, I choose to wear black
because it insists that everyone see me
without the distractions of coral or magenta.
I am that woman in plain black shirt.
I continue to wear my black hair long,
gather in it red strands from the sun,
use black to measure the forest of colors
even in my dark eyes,
and in this skin which browns
like warm sienna earth.

4

inside a windowless black night
a woman holds onto the moon,
its creamy whiteness filtering out
of the steady dark eye,
her shadow pressing the light as surely
as a woman beginning to know who she is
and what cannot be separated from her—
one cradle of moon and hands.

5

a child begins with no notion of black.
she is taught about the unknown—
it is impure and cannot be tolerated.

she comes from a darkskinned race
and a country where everyone already knows
too much about her.
but she won't die, no matter.

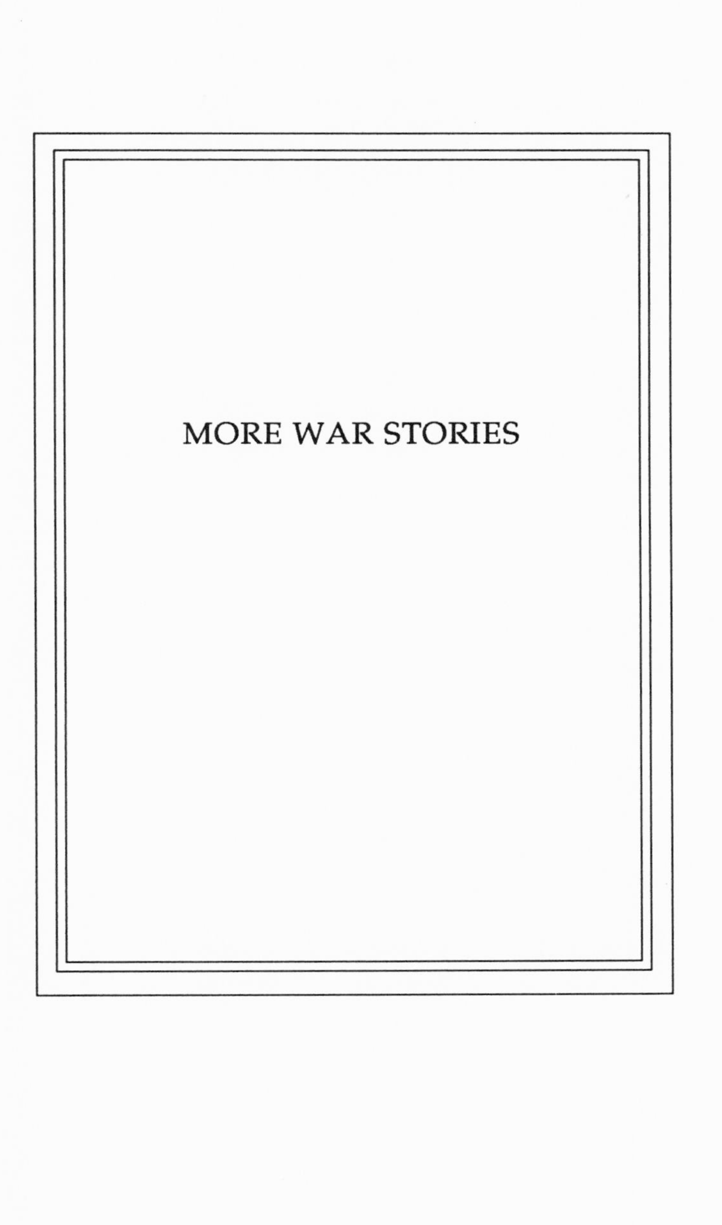

MORE WAR STORIES

DID YOU HEAR WHAT HAPPENED TO MO?

It's a twenty foot fall
from his window—
when Mo fell to the ground,
we all thought this is where
he would want to die,
right on the cement sidewalk
facing the Alan Hotel,
built for new arrivals
back in the twenties,
young issei farmers
smiling and moustached
in starched white shirts,
or the migrant workers waiting
to harvest the next crop of beans,
and there were always men like Mo,
fed up living on the outside.
Mo came back to the one place
he felt he belonged,
found a one-room apartment
in the Alan Hotel,
where he watched how big money from Japan
was tearing the old community,
block by block,
all the tiny fish markets, Buddhist
temples, mom & pop stores
replaced by highrise hotels,

medical buildings, exclusive gift shops
selling Italian handbags, French perfumes,
City Hall praising its
so-called redevelopment.
But Mo didn't die—
some say the PCP had already
killed his pain,
I heard he landed on a Skid Row white man
who screamed,
"God's punishing me now
with this goddamned slanteyed angel,
the whole country bein' taken over."
But Mo keeps on living
because he just may be the most stubborn
man around, next to Stanley Yamashiro,
and no twenty foot fall can stop his
warning how everything can be taken
if we let them.
Last time I checked
Mo was still out there talking
though the Alan Hotel is gone.

NEAR ROSCOE AND COLDWATER
(the Northeast San Fernando Valley, 1985)

i. Sunday

This is a busy corner.
Truckdrivers, businessmen, lowriders,
all slow down to view
the building of the Thai temple.
On the vacant lot next to gas stations
and a closed down 7-ll, the roof of gold appears.
Barefoot men in orange robes
plant grass and small shade trees.
Every Sunday immigrants drive in,
they follow the light
reflected in the golden roof.
I hear chanting sounds and afterwards
the easy laughter of families
cooking lunch on outdoor grills.
They fill the neighborhood with Eastern scents,
above the car fumes and dry weed.

ii. Boy's Story

He is eighteen and no matter
how many times I mispronounce his name,
he always smiles, an old man's face.
I am his only Asian teacher
since he left Kampuchea.
I've read, argued, marched,

and now after seeing a film about the war,
I have the audacity to ask what he knows.
"My father killed by Khymer Rouge.
Brother killed too. Mother escaped,"
but he may never find her.
Still smiling, he tells me about
his new car. Now and then I see him,
cruising Victory Boulevard.

iii. The Crossing

Morning traffic has stopped.
A line of honking cars,
capable of crushing the small woman.
She is stuck at the railroad crossing,
the shopping cart of used cans and rags
too heavy for her thin body.
She looks like the Vietnamese grandmothers
I've seen so often in photographs,
especially her eyes
which tend
caravans of old men and babies.
Tireless eyes keeping vigil
in the seconds of animal silence, before
each approaching assault.
Drivers yell as she talks to herself
in her own language, but everyone watches
eyes that can sift
through earth, bone, metal, blood,
knowing which fragments to save.

THE SAME MONTH THEY BOMBED CAMBODIA

— for Mary and John Kao

We open the street door,
three floors up over a noodle factory,
to a perfume thickened by frying things,
sweet sauces, freshly cut ducks and hens,
hot oil smells collide with leaking sewage pipes,
the stink from ten day garbage that won't be collected.
And the perfume still thickens—
the sesame scent of noodles
fills these narrow streets and air pockets
left between too many bodies,
sidewalks breathing oldness, poverty, sweat,
and new immigrant hustle.

A homemade poster— come to a health fair—
free pap smear...t.b. tests...child care provided.
This is how it could be, buy our newspaper and find out.

A cha shiu bao, the biggest I've ever eaten.

A Lower Eastside cockroach, the biggest I've seen—
lights switched on, my foot threatens, it refuses to run,
I learn to go to the bathroom with eyes closed.

A late night drinkoff— while we argue RCP, IWK, ASG,
and other wellknown initials, Charlie sings genocide.

China has millions, Japan its Sonies and Datsuns,
we'll be the scapegoat again, or we could move,
start new like our grandparents.

A book from Soho fashioned by Ting,
his penis on every third page— red, blue, pink, green.

A recipe for black beans on rice, copied from
the Cuban who goes by the name Jorge Chan.

An afternoon watching painters on flying ladders
free the entire face of the ghetto skyscraper—
their favorite subjects the old women,
also peasant mothers wearing sandals and rifles.

A melody of kid chatter, white hair gossip,
each dialect smoothly inflected. Flirting talk,
bickering talk, cursing crying laughing talk,
some even think we belong,
look hard when we can't answer.

A bargain platter of spicy beef with peppers,
only $2.95— no charge for dinner show—
waiters jump white man who won't stop yelling chinks.

A walk towards Times Square with our Asian contingent,
no one warns us about the horses— we scatter,
the man with moustache and nightstick picks me.
I have long black hair like the Cambodians.

MAIL ORDER

You can order anything you want in America. I got my bride in a catalog of love. Gorgeous little thing from the Phillipines, so delicate I can lift her up with one arm. I got laid for the first time in Saigon, back in 67, and after that many more times in Saigon, Manila, and Singapore. After that I couldn't stop thinking about those sweet doll faces. Don't get me wrong, I still like blue eyes and blond hair. And no one admires long made-in-America legs more than me. But a man can't live anymore with his own women. This wife of mine never talks back. 'Course, she can't speak too much English yet, but what she doesn't know can't hurt her. She keeps my house clean, doesn't complain when I stay out too late, does anything I ask in bed. I've never been treated so well by any American woman. The wife says she'll always be grateful I chose her from the hundreds of beautiful photographs. Imagine my luck too— after my first letter she already knew she loved me. Says she always dreamed of coming here and marrying a man just like me. Dependable as a Japanese car, she is worth every dollar I paid.

THEY ALWAYS TRAVEL WITH HENCHMEN

As they enter our sleepy towns,
making the final escape from Eastern palaces—
these fat merchants, former landloreds, ex-
generals and toppled president's wives
who arrive with money in their pockets,
their suitcases crammed with antique jade,
secret bank accounts, incriminating papers
as additional insurance.

They come here in the middle of the night,
tell us to think of them as ordinary now—
simple fishermen and small investors
who can never permit us to marry their children
and continue to sleep with unclosed eyes.
Their lives have always demanded this.

FORTUNE COOKIE BLUES

i

The way I hear it, Chinese fortune cookies
are about as authentic
as Hollywood's Charlie Chan,
only this story has a better twist
(not slant) to it.
They were concocted by some shrewd issei
who came over on a Japanese freighter.
He probably borrowed the idea—
the Chinese I know say any invention
can be traced back to the Middle Kingdom,
and everyone knows that Japanese
are called great imitators.
So this issei's son opens a little bakery
after their release
from that barbed wire camp.
They made an instant fortune conning
Americans whose idea of real Chinese food
is chop suey— and dessert,
a piece of Confucian wisdom
ingeniously packaged in one small,
mysterious cookie.

ii

My father's father named his third son Star,
just like he named the nursery
which made him rich during the Thirties.
Some say Grandpa's old hands were magical,
breeding lush red camellias and pink azaleas
for species and shadings not yet named.
Stiff branches of juniper bent with ease
wherever his hands led them.
But Star died before turning sixteen,
and all of Grandpa's land, flowers,
secrets he discovered in the soil
and carefully recorded in diaries
were left to the remaining children—
whose hands were never magical.

iii

I wonder if gambling is passed on
in the blood, especially for Japanese.
What other little country would dare
attack at Pearl Harbor? What forces
an American minority, falsely imprisoned
as traitors, to enlist in the Army,
calling ourselves "Go for Broke"—
this nisei counterpart to kamikaze?
Can a defeated people,
bombed at Hiroshima and Nagasaki,

recover in just one generation?
In the fifth grade Barney Barnes,
whose mother was half Cherokee,
asked me about World War II movies,
"Which side do you cheer for?"
I was sure he'd betrayed me.
Ten years later he died in 'Nam.

iv

Before I didn't take fortune-telling seriously,
didn't know my ancestors tied paper wishes onto trees,
thin ribbons catching the wind,
whispering messages to the dead,
the living confident that even these tiny paper flags
would not go unnoticed by the gods.

v

There's a nisei woman three blocks away.
Her husband gambled in the big time,
died suddenly when he couldn't pay up.
Now she lives in her grey Mercedes Benz,
her home cluttered with clothing and newspapers.
She parks on the land he left her,
land worth millions now,
where she eats and sleeps,
refusing to leave her car,
always keeping one eye on her rearview mirror.

v

My son grows up in a different time.
He can't be singled out like I was,
the only Japanese in a small WASP town.
Too many of us now to bully anymore.
I should be happy for him.
But just last week two kids on bikes
circled me with "Ching Chong" insults,
and nothing I said could make them see me.

HARVEST

TELL ME ABOUT THE LAUGHTER OF ANGELS

It is not so easy to live on the earth
as an angel.

—Richard Jackson

You tell me you'll reveal why birds fly off
without warning from telephone wires,
and I want to believe in that sudden motion,
when lightning or god or plain dumb luck
will finally slap me back to my senses,
or give me the full relief of my delusions.

Let me close my eyes and come back
with one less question, without this need to know
the real meaning of the fish who belongs
in water but insists on growing feet,
about the persistence inside this wingless bird
who longs to remember flying in her dreams.

Should I begin with nothing more than
the grand sameness of sky, blue and relentless,
even when I keep losing count
of the unnamed children, dying
we're all of us helping to bury?
After so much weeping, is the wind which
scratches just outside my door unmoved?

Maybe the trick is in not trying so hard,
to give up on the notion of evil
or the possibility of sanity without murder.
Whose eyes are these growing large
in the dark? Even during sleep
I feel them flickering,
their small incessant pulse under eyelids
whose fragile covering of flesh cannot
keep out the light.

My eyes want to sink so far into the body
that no light will come in.
Let me sleep like a child again,
feel my way back inside
the quiet darkness which separates stars.
Maybe then I can join you in praying
we each find the angels in our lives.
Now, when I can't hear the laughter of angels,
I will not forget the sound of waves,
a sweet memory of wings of seaweed,
tiny green leaf, all the fish
who leap from the surface of moist skin
into a sky charred violet and orange.
Let me know it is enough to feel the sheer weight
of the small hand still opening in my own,
to accept these bits of wing and blood
falling back to the water are one.

FROM A CEREMONY REPEATED

I wear onyx and silver on my dark arms.
And silence fills my house
as I hold a smooth, black pebble
in my upturned palm.
There are stories I was never told—
only a silk kimono
passed on to me in an antique box,
while the scent of incense and powder
lingers in the robe's black folds.
Or the repeated glimpse of a woman
unknotting her long black hair,
her blood in mine—
the fragile knotting which ties me
to all the darkhaired women
who recognize my name.

The farmer's wife at her loom, an unknown potter
at her wheel. Patches of night uncover
spinning sounds. I feel the wetness of black mountain clay.
On my table I place this delicate container for pine
as I invent rituals without words—
to acknowledge this stranger whose hands
adorn my table with her craft.

I use blackness as a way back in,
the sound of water on water.

I celebrate a summer night which gave itself to me—
black tropical sky and a moon behind clouds
when I knew I'd stopped wanting a husband,
and loving him from a deeper place
could finally let each of us go.

These small ceremonies repeated in gesture—
the swirl of water and ink, like a calligrapher
moving black inside white.
I am learning the balance of darkness to light,
how the practiced flicker of fingers and wrist can reveal
a world. I need to keep seeing
my own child's eyes are small, black stones,
which I once carried in my hands.
Need to watch him in sleep, his young lashes
resting soft and straight like an unused brush.
And each day to notice
all the life which still grows in me—
the trembling warm skin under this single crow's wing.

FROM AN UTAGAWA PRINT: GEISHAS PARADING

i: Seven Robes

A child holds the trailing hem
of a geisha's robes, listening to the rustle
of silk and snow, as the woman steps
slowly in high, black lacquered slippers.

This street is full of women—
there are no men here, though the child
has seen men hiding in the thick
folds of a woman's seven robes.

ii: With Blue Flowers in Her Hair

A girl has been chosen
to follow the woman who powders her neck,
to be trained in the intricacies
of seduction, how to layer the body
in silk, letting the hand
pause against the kimono's
fine coarseness, every eye
aroused by pink and red peonies,
giant yellow chrysanthemums,
delicate geometrics woven in
jade, turquoise, and plum,
grey winter birds on a sleeve of black sky.

With blue flowers in her hair, a girl
will learn how some men enjoy the slow
sliding off of robes, unhurried
dreaming from a warm, white place.

INAKA/ COUNTRY GIRL

I'd recognize him by the white suit
he wears every night. Pachuco stance.
Nothing rushed. Leans back into a stride
that boys learn early on the streets.
Keeps his eyes well hidden behind shades.

No question he's a buddhahead—
those thick bushido eyebrows,
his straight black hair combed high and back,
a casual wisp against the pale forehead.

Reminds me of the young Mifune
when he played a Tokyo gangster.
Only this man's dangerous in a different way.
Dressed in his all white suit,
he sits outside a club on Kapiolani.
Knows just how fine he looks tonight.
Everything about him is deliberate—
the carefully groomed beard and moustache,
a striped bow tie, even the zoris on his feet.

I'm just another small town girl
with not much time left, telling myself
there's nothing to be afraid of—
he's only smiling at me, wearing that silly

orange plastic lei around his neck,
a guitar resting on his legs,
hands in a half strum, ready.

---

bushido: samurai-like

zoris: Japanese slippers

Mifune: popular Japanese actor, Toshiro Mifune

YOU COME FROM ST. LOUIS

You don't even like the idea of raw fish.
I'm eating more meat now and no longer get mad
when you repeat jokes about women's odor
resembling something ancient and overwhelming from the sea.
As for me, I'm not so different from my Japanese ancestors,
I love to breathe in the smell of kelp, salt breeze,
and fishermen's hands.

You belong to the flatlands, those corn and wheat plains
where you never learned to swim
and only trusted a well cooked slab of cow or pig,
salted, coated in flour or dipped in chili and tabasco sauce,
baked for hours and hours in your mother's oven.
What do you taste when you taste me?
I know your skin's flavor and scent now
and it stays sweet on my tongue.

With a non-Southern accent you still say you-all,
your once Irish masters' names
on both your mother's and father's sides.
Your history is still too recent
for my family, ashamed
when a daughter of theirs could turn
to a man so far outside their own
definition of love or even lust.
There is nothing more I can say to them,

so I'll listen with you to a slow saxophone.
Comfortable in our silence after making love,
this dim light in the bedroom reveals
the dark and pale of our limbs resting as one,
and I can feel how much harder
your heart beats, mine keeping its own time,
in this strangely syncopated American dance.

CHRYSANTHEMUM ROCK

I ask my son what he knows about stones.
Unlike me, has he learned some simple geology?
But he can't answer and asks why I'm so curious.
I tell him I've just seen a remarkable rock—
its burnished surface a lustrous dark brown,
covered with tiny pink markings, distinctly
patterned like chrysanthemum petals.
It was found in Japan and could even be magical,
these delicate flowers appearing to grow within stone.
Perhaps some ancient hand painted the chrysanthemums
with an indelible ink which has withstood
centuries of rain and wind.
My son still ponders his mother's fascination
for a rock, mumbling again about my weirdness.
I don't tell him about all the times I've depended
on stones. How much I return to them,
praying they'll offer me some clue, some quiet
reassurance when I'm tired of living inside my own
despair. I haven't shown my son
how often my poems arise out of stones—
in the silence of a husband, the memory
of a dry, California riverbed where my grandfather
stood listening to the murmur of water, or in the eyes
of the men in my life, including this child.
I tell him how much I love small, black stones
but not that I'm talking to them, now
that I've lost hold of a lover again.

My favorite rock is the flat black oval I found
at Pismo Beach. Placing it in my palm,
I press its cool skin against mine.
I hear something far away breaking—
and a hardening inside which I can't stop.
I return the stone to my basket of beach pebbles,
recalling the morning I gathered them,
carrying as many as I could in my two cupped hands—
much like the way I take in love.
Then I hand my son what looks like an ordinary
grey stone, but in the shape of a lopsided heart,
repeating, "Isn't this a wonderful find?".

LETTUCE AND STRAWBERRIES

our grandfathers could
move their hands beneath land
no one else wanted—
until it breathed for them.
everything they touched bore fruit—
even at night, that moist, dark field.

HARVEST

1. orchid

behind Ikeda's house
it is always cool,
smell of damp soil,
the ripple of fat koi
through a garden pond,
shelves of purple orchids
forming thick boundaries
against a city.
he buys a new plant every year,
ships it in from Hawaii.
he says a single orchid
yields one hundred more,
all shaded differently,
though offspring
from one flower.

so Ikeda watches
as each new bloom unfolds,
naming only the most unusual—
Kaoru, on the second tier,
pale and edged in maroon;
or Lynn, yellow and lavender,
after his third child.
every woman in his large family
will have her own orchid,

though he is in no hurry—
names will not be given carelessly.

he is a nisei gardener
with six grown daughters and sons.
this man knows about water and shade,
likes to pamper his hands
with small, wet things.
after work he sits
outside his house,
waits for evening to begin,
orchids surrounding him
like dark, sturdy fingers
while he listens again
to the breathing of children.

2. plum

still bitter
the plum's red skin,
its fruit pale and hard;
but wait until late June
when the days are long—
its firm skin will turn
dark as blood,
juice pressing against
the thin membrane.

when a plum ripens
we are given
only three or four days
to eat its sweet pulp.
if we aren't watching closely,
it must fall to the ground,
the smooth skin torn,
no longer able to contain
what is meant
for summer tasting.

3. peony

her blood is thicker
each month the flow heavy, almost purple,
like the lips of her womb,
or just after her baby was born,
his curled grey sack
bursting into arms and kicks,
a noisy violet red.
this woman is older now—
no longer at war,
everything about her body—
the unfilled nipples, her smell,
all seem so close,
she feels so much heat.

4. iris

Ikeda brings iris
into his room,
calls it shobu,
places long, slender leaves
in bath water
for healing
in the Japanese custom,
a flower standing straight
on its stalk,
upright for days,
though its edges are soft—
bending back purple,
stirring the light
with one eye.

---

koi: carp

shobu: iris

A PINCH OF BONITO

daddy used to bring us fish
from Ensenada
albacore, Spanish mackeral,
blue fin tuna caught the day before.

he brought them home
already iced then wrapped in newspaper
he piled them in our kitchen sink
removed fins, head, skin
knew where to find the firmest meat
easy to slice
never too thick
with his sharp knife angled
just so.

when he sat at the dinner table
with two daughters and a wife
he talked and talked
not about the size of his latest catch
not even about us.

he didn't know
what to do with his hands
brown, calloused hands
more accustomed to hold things
which can be pulled out of salt water,

or coaxed out of soil
with enough water and light.
he thought he needed to fill the air
with his ideas.

I liked the silence
once we started to eat—
the sashimi so smooth
on our tongues,
our thin wood hashi
tapping lightly against china
as we scooped in
each mouthful of rice.

in winter
when it was too cold
for deep sea fishing
daddy bought dried bonito—
hard as bone,
its skin a dark crust.
he kept it in a strange wooden box
which came from Japan.

he would grip the bonito
in his right fist,
shaving its body
back and forth
against the inset blade.
press down, then back
his hand never breaking
its rhythm.

when he was ready
he'd let us open a magic drawer—
pale orange curls
with a salty fragrance.
he told us "a pinch of bonito
is all you need"
and he never knew
this would have been enough.

we're older now
but daddy still likes to do
all the talking
and we answer him like we did
as children
with small sucking noises,
the chawans cupped in our palms
almost touching our chins,
the steam from hot tea
rising into pores
as we refill our bellies
with rice and bonito,
only lately more certain
how much can pass
through a father's hands.

---

hashi: chopsticks

chawans: rice bowls

RICE PLANTING

In the sky at night
Stars known as the "rice basket,"
Blossom like flowers,
All day I make rice baskets;
At night I view these flowers.
—16th c. Japanese tanka

Even my mother has taught herself
to acquire the taste of butter & bread,
but I refuse. Every night I must make
two cups of rice—
after washing the grains,
the level of water measured exactly,
only as high as the first groove
on my third finger.
This is essential,
for Japanese rice is wetter than others.
We say Chinese rice falls apart
too easily (they say ours is too sticky).
A newleywed bride has ruined many meals
by a rice too dry or too moist.

I plan every dinner around rice.
I know it's a starch like potatoes or noodles,
but I'm sure rice has so many more uses.
I can cook it with any meat,
fish, or casserole. I even serve rice with spaghetti.

And leftover rice is just as good—
fried with last night's scraps,
or the cold rice I reheat with tea,
then sprinkle with bonito shavings,
to become a hot soup
to be slurped the next day.

Of course there's the vinegared rice
that's the basis for sushi,
then on special occasions
a wine colored rice
flavored with dark red azuki beans.
Rice goes in our Thanksgiving stuffing,
it's a cracker for munching with beer,
and pounded, rice can be molded
into New Year's mochi cakes
or sweetened for manju
in pink and white stripes.

When we go to the mountains or beach,
the best part of the trip is our picnic lunch—
triangles and spool shapes of rice,
covered with roasted sesame seeds
or in green and black wrappers of dried seaweed.
These onigiri always go well with fried
chicken or slices of ham.

If I'm sick, mother boils
a heavy rice gruel which will
settle my stomach.

And when we don't feel like cooking
there's that breakfast rice
which can only be ordered in Buddhahead
towns, like Honolulu or Gardena—
rice heaped on a platter,
two eggs over easy,
your choice of Portuguese sausage,
bacon, or Chinese roast pork—
a typical Japanese American meal.

I can remember when I couldn't boast
like this about rice. My father told us
the upper classes never
ate rice with their main course
like we did. Now I can even put rice
in my son's sack lunches—
when I ask him again if friends joke or stare,
I am back in the sixth grade
at my all white school,
in a less sophisticated time before sushi
became just another California fast food.

There is also the rice not eaten.
Moistened and mashed it's reliable glue.
Uncooked it's a good luck sign
to be thrown at weddings.
When rice is fermented as sake,
it's served chilled in wood boxes
with lemon and ice,

or so hot it melts the body
and is likely to make me dance and sing.
In craftsman's hands it's passed on
as a fine rice paper,
barely transparent and suited for lanterns
or poems brushed in ink.

But above all rice is a plain people's food.
Before temples and imperial palaces,
my peasant ancestors planted
until the land and grain were the harvest,
the rhythm we lived by.
Rice is the staple of farmers and monks—
nothing is wasted.
It has fed me on many long journeys—
and though my family no longer grows rice
and our women no longer bend
to a rice planting song,
I am thankful when my own son
from the fourth generation
tells me he's hungry and smiles
when I hand him a riceball
the size of my fist.